ONE CLEAN FEATHER

poems by

Julia Caroline Knowlton

Finishing Line Press
Georgetown, Kentucky

ONE CLEAN FEATHER

ACKNOWLEDGMENTS

I wish to thank the editors of the following journals, in which some of these
poems originally appeared: *Ekphrastic Review* (Afternoon in the Louvre),
Eunoia Review (Le Bonheur), *Peacock Journal* (To the Next Man I will Love),
PHEMME (Safety Sonnet), *Rat's Ass Review* (When we Make Love), *Raw
Art Review* (La Cravate, About Juliet, The Kiss, Eternal Idol), and *Roanoke
Review* (Postcards from Paris).

"Persistent Wish" and "Postcard from Paris" originally appeared in my 2018
chapbook, *Café of Unintelligible Desire* (Alice Greene & Company). Thank
you to Jill Peek for permission to reprint.

Publisher: Leah Maines
Editor: Christen Kincaid
Cover Art: Claire De Pree
Author Photo: Julia Caroline Knowlton
Cover Design: Elizabeth Maines McCleavy

Printed in the USA on acid-free paper.
Order online: www.finishinglinepress.com
also available on amazon.com

Author inquiries and mail orders:
Finishing Line Press
P. O. Box 1626
Georgetown, Kentucky 40324
U. S. A.

Table of Contents

For my family—biological & chosen.

"Hope" is the thing with feathers—
That perches in the soul—
And sings the tune without the words—
And never stops—at all—

—Emily Dickinson

PART ONE:

One Clean Feather: A Memoir

I do not write this for myself.

(I cannot even read this, since I've already died.)

No, I write this for you—& you & you & you.

All around me, more endings in fire & ice

color & letter forever in the air   see how they fly & fly

What sea do we sing for

                or pure we weep

A video (gone viral) about consent

uses tea as an analogy:

do you want some tea?

No thank you.

I thought maybe I did before, but now I do not.

No really, I insist.

Are you nobody?

Me too too.

The letter *em*: always m for mom

or (do you remember) auntie Em   there is no place like home

but you can't go home again

Click your ruby slippers & throw your bricks of gold.

Where over the rainbow   fly why can't I

The letter ee—sound of every scream

but not the nice ice cream scream

The first time it happened

I was twelve years old   first week of junior high

Climbing stairs on my way to class

a male hand thrust   in between my thighs

forceful, grabbing me there, metal stairwell filled with dozens of kids—

backpacks & gum snapping & laughing.

I froze. Shame coiled in my throat; a snake made of ice.

Shock spooled me into silence: safe became unsafe.

There was no telling who it was.

Had I been entirely innocent until then?

trust of a child   blush of open roses

How was school, my mother asked at home, that afternoon.

                                        It was fine, I said.

I filed it away in my mind:

cold, metal filing cabinet of recollection.

Not the *could have been worse* file.

Not the *was it really that bad* file.

I was far too young for that: so naïve

still a girl in cotton shoes   stuffed animals on my bed

It was the hidden, silent

there is just no way to understand this file.

Mouth with no tongue.   Mouth with no teeth.

Mouth with no tongue. Mouth with no teeth.

The next time, I was sweet sixteen:

my date on top of me in a van, sour beer breath,

his strength and my repeating no.

He was a rich kid.   Like he owned the world.

My mother had bought me a new dress for that dance;

it was white dotted swiss with a pale blue, satin belt.

I see the lace hem in between these words.

He had blue eyes, too.   Neon streetlights stared.

Telling my parents nothing.   Then becoming so quiet.

Realizing internally oh okay, I see—so this is how it's going to have to be.

a rose is a rose is a rose is a rose
boys will be boys will be boys will be boys
a rose is a rose is a rose is a rose
boys will be boys will be boys will be boys
a rose is a rose is a rose is a rose
boys will be boys will be boys will be boys
a rose is a rose is a rose is a rose
boys will be boys will be boys will be boys
a rose is a rose is a rose is a rose
boys will be boys will be boys will be boys
a rose is a rose is a rose is a rose
boys will be boys will be boys will be boys
a rose is a rose is a rose is a rose
boys will be boys will be boys will be boys

then illness barreled in—

anorexia

a textbook case   as if on cue

because really   why would I not have desired

to disappear   five foot ten only   115

the snow drift more appealing than the field fat with grain

the silence more meaningful than any melody ever written

I lived my own disappearance   quieter than quiet

perfection you see   is the presence of absence

pure air or   a real snow angel

now I've managed it   nothing can hurt me

I fell in love at seventeen.   He heard why I disappeared.

Every word we said became a cloud   gentle, gentle

I gave him my virginity one night.   My parents were away.

While we slept, his buddies toilet-papered the trees—

filmy white tissue hung in branches tight with buds

Soon after, he went to one elite college, I went to another.

Years later I looked for him   cloud after cloud

Since safe was unsafe   I went to live in books—

leaving home for English & French at university.

British lit: neither Woolf nor Austen were ever assigned.

No Brontës. Do not cross over this grass on the quad.

French lit: no Colette, no Sand, no Simone de Beauvoir.

(Breton & all the rest—woman an object   *objet trouvé*)

Heavy lead canon balls from the canon.   Catching them like medicine balls:

Tristam Shandy Tom Jones Moby Dick well you get the idea

No writer of color.   Not even a token.

I was a good girl & read them all.

I was a good girl & revered them all.

Rolled linen trousers & eating a peach.

The note explaining the empty bowl with no plums.

Ladies lounging in peignoirs

like women painted by Whistler

their nights of starry hysteria

hyacinths of silence   wet with rain

So this is how it is, okay.   I would find them on my own.

I found Sexton but she was already gone.

I found Plath but she was already gone.

Anne wrapped in her mother's fur & liquor

sleeping forever in the fumes

Sylvia, her myth larger than her truth

the towel rolled forever under that door

Woolf too—

her body river flowers, Ophelia-like

I was looking for sisters   mothers

mouth with no tongue, mouth with no teeth

hands without hands

I found Edna   empty house   booze & morphine

gone there   crumpled in a heap at the bottom stair

Emily in her white gown upstairs in cold air—

        hungry for more

had she read

every blade of grass?   ships of clouds on seas of clouds

fat fly buzzing buzzing   as she died

(what to do   what to do)

thin recluse   empty bowl no more plums

all the tiny buttons on her dress

all the tiny buttons on her shoes

Then I found women living

Rich diving into the wreck

Angelou singing how the caged bird sings

Warm arms and warmer eyes

At a reading one hot August night I met Gwendolyn Brooks

she signed my book   while I asked her for a line of life

she looked me down deep in the eyes

told me to read   told me to write

the mouth finding sound

hand holding a hand   that gift, one moment one night

A woman like a bird in an oil spill:

feathers all gunked up with refuse & grease

matted & bent   grounded

(if she is lucky, she flew once as a girl   so at least she can recall)

her only hope is to get those feathers cleaned

it can be done, but a bird cannot do it all alone

safety sonnet

know exactly where you parked/carry car keys in your hand
walk confidently staring straight ahead/don't walk alone at night
if you drink order your own /don't leave your drink out of sight
only exercise indoors /only meet new date in public
text friends at beginning & end of new date/carry pepper spray or mace
make assertive eye contact (don't look scared)/park close to exits in parking decks
carry bag close to your body/wear shoes that will allow you to run
if you are followed cross the street/if you wear a short skirt
if you wear heels/if you wear a low-cut blouse/if you ever wear red
take a self-defense class/stay in your car doors locked while pumping gas
don't give out your number/don't leave any windows open
be aware of your surroundings at all times/do you know what you are doing
but above all don't look scared (don't look scared) (don't look scared)
but above all don't look scared (don't look scared) (don't look scared)

The next time it happened   I was a waitress
on an island resort, saving my tips to go to Paris.
Boss man gave the so-called pretty girls dinner shift:
more cocktails, bigger bills, bigger tips.
One night, late, as I was carrying salad bar trays
a line cook followed me into a walk-in deep freezer
He slammed me against the back wall
absolutely no light pitch black he grabbed and forced
my light breasts my light hips he assaulted me hard
his weasel voice, his moustache a row of black flies
once again I broke free   those minutes last forever
(it has been thirty years & still I regularly flash back)
why did I not report it   why did I not report it
why do we not report it   this is the end of this sonnet

When I stopped eating, I started drinking.

No need to mess with that chaos here.

Let's just say it was a thirty-year detour.

Decades later, after the havoc I wrought,

I quit the dead-end wine habit. Just in time.

(like I said at the beginning—I cannot even read

what I am writing, since I've already died)

Paris, France   healing beauty   *une merveille*

not a city of big shoulders   but a city of soft shoulders

Notre Dame like a lady's stone gown

eternal swell of the steely Seine

more grace than I had ever imagined

long winter afternoons on my own in the Louvre

chocolat chaud   pure music of French

damp cobblestone streets & wrought iron balconies

something all mine   to taste, to say

One perfect, winter afternoon in the Louvre

I stood in front of Manet's *Le Déjeuner sur l'herbe*

for almost an hour.   Nude woman

seated closely with two clothed men.

Their legs and feet intertwined.   His black shoe

not quite touching her ivory statue foot.

Some kind of old illusion—*ménage à trois.*

Her direct gaze, yes—depth of brown eyes!

Blue ribbon on straw hat. Spilled fruit on the grass.

Prostitute or goddess?   Well, that's all of us.

Institut Charles V   Université de Paris Diderot

A literature class taught in English

Outside, a warm March rain.

My Irish professor asked me to read aloud—

Katherine Mansfield: The Garden Party

garden roses became words   words became archangels

(a place in constant shade of roses

has made this page now   closed off from death)

I could not believe my good fortune, studying a female writer

one formally assigned   what a glorious taste   otherworldly

I floated down the *rue des Écoles*, ethereal

all you need to begin is one clean feather

One afternoon in Paris as I was walking along the Seine

a black limousine glided fully onto the curb, trapping me against the *quai*.

A man emerged from the back; told his driver to wait.

Would I go out to lunch with him.

His hands in his pants pockets.   His head cocked.

No, no. Go away. *Allez vous-en! Laissez-moi tranquille.*

I spoke French well enough to make it all go away.

Can't I just walk in peace, think in peace.

                    Can't I just have space.

I wept when I left Paris.   I should never have left.

(If you find a place where you can fly, make it your nest.)

Soon after, I became a bride.   Now comes a big silence:

blank paper of regret.   (We should have known all along.)

Twice a mother: two perfect daughters—a song, another song.

So much of writing is trying to right what went wrong.

After years like reams & reams of blank paper

our marriage reached its dead end

because love turned into strife

death so often called a loss of life

I read Sylvia   *dying is an art*

I read Anne   her desire to die

was *warmer than oil or water*

For years I drank two bottles of wine a day

drove drunk   paid the price

broke my ribs   broke your hearts

It is not that I almost died   I did die

Then I got sober   Now I stay sober

Light in the morning   Light at night

Hand in hand   Mouth finding sound

On every tongue the faint snow of prayer

Before I got sober   it happened two more times

One: a former student set me up with a professor

On the second date he tried to rape me

He was so forceful, so much stronger than me

In front of his fireplace, on the floor, it was the holidays

On the first date I met him in a public place   as instructed for safety

On the second date I brought my own car   as instructed for safety

He bruised my mouth black & blue   that bruise never goes away

Two: raped by a man in AA

He said that night he had given up on getting sober

He had come to change the deadbolt on my door

He had hooked tall beers on his toolbelt with his tools

I want to say that was the last time   eight years ago

but you never know   just last week I was on my way to work

minding my own business, pumping gas

being aware of my surroundings just as we know we do

looked down for one moment & suddenly *that feeling* again

a man drove up in his car six inches away from me

"Ma'am I just want to tell you you're a beautiful woman;

I don't mean any harm."   his low voice   danger of intrusion

that look in his eyes   can't we just fill our tanks in peace

I was so rattled I pulled the pump out too soon   spilled gas all over me

as he drove away   it puddled on the ground

iridescent in early morning light

                                        all the colors of the rainbow

How to clean your grimy, oil-soaked feathers:

find the right person to help you

allow yourself to be held gently in mild soap

the soap can be nature it can be art it can be god

be patient, patriarchy is so incredibly dirty

it takes a very long time: soul mind & body

the only way to learn to trust is to trust

the only way to learn to hope is to hope

mighty feather pen

quiet quill   wet wet ink

ink black & blue   last but not least

weightless power   the *nom de plume*

Isn't it   remarkable how women wear feathers—

on hats in the loveliest of colors   like royal blue

or bold boas—so bright

Sunday going to church or

Strutting down the runway

or simply plump in down coats   staying warm

pretty plumage   hoping hoping

birds with clipped wings wanting to fly

impossibly floating   right here

above all of the hurt

PART TWO:

Eternal Idol

Song

Your lust for color arrests

me. Our wondering in words—

angel, *chaleur, rouge, violet*—

Lulls me out of waking sleep.

The quest in your voice

is beyond anything named.

(Surely your strong hands

once   were doves)

You

Have brown eyes & call me by name.

In curves of words, you are mine.

We might be one but for the taking.

Light suspends us constant, apart.

Stillborn desire of tomb, shadow throne.

When We Make Love

When we make love, just what kind of love

are we making; the kind where you wear black

and I wear white, and we float near blue flowers

in a sky, in a painting? Or the kind where we walk

down a city street in tweed coats, crunching autumn

leaves under our feet, then go our separate ways?

I do not know where I go when your force washes through me.

I know that all emotion is mere water, falling in more water.

Who can say what hidden stones might be moved.

Who can say what part of the wet ground might stay.

Kimono Exhibit at the Met

We talk of nothing as we come and go,

standing before each glass-cased kimono.

A red-lipped lover covers her heart,

embroidered men push a wooden cart.

Scenes of tea and intimacy compete

with swords of betrayal and deceit.

Mandarin oranges meet dragon breath

as each silk empires love and death.

And when we leave the Metropolitan

I start to retreat from you yet again.

Standing Nude

Deep within the passing of this sole

true moment, all becomes silence of space

& conversation of color. The world

turns mild as it opens and effaces.

I gladly disappear into untold lines

traced by our story's uncertainty of light.

You sketch movement across a virgin surface—

bodiless, your pen scratching toward flight.

Reclining Nude

<<Fugitive beauté>>

Baudelaire

Here she is, in memory's pose—the indolent one,

the passer-by who met a poet's gaze & then

returned to her mind's repose, already knowing

what he dared to imagine, placing her hand to hat

& looking quickly away. Beyond brim of chapeau,

end of the bed, hem of her dress & linen's lace edge,

eternal curves of the reclining nude. The model paid

an hourly wage. Just glad to lie down in mid-afternoon.

In her mind, *will this be over soon.*

Eternal Idol

Lips eclipse in cool resistance of stone—

His insistence humbled by the enigma

of her curves. As she bends to his need,

the arc of her heart surpasses it. She feels

his questions enter & become her own.

This is their communion

                          beyond his animal grasp.

Her eyes close—flowers offered

                          with no promise of return.

Tiny Ars Poetica

Every vow means exile.

Words lose worth.

Is your death my death?

Our disappearance into earth.

Persistent Wish

I want to be nobody, too—

a bright voice perfectly freed from the body.

Blue shadow snow. Curled air between

a pair of winged things. Whirling cold flight.

To find the end, sooner rather than later—

sharp as silver, clean & stunning.

To the Next Man I will Love

Why would I even think of you?

You with no name,

you with your hair of stone.

And yet I keep preparing myself:

eating my golden apples,

washing my faraway feet.

About Juliet

It must have been winter when her heart

became a firmament & her countenance, a dove.

(Love disobeys duty; stop before you start.)

I only know my page of night, signifying nothing

over & over again. But she made new meaning

when she graced her forbidden balcony in Verona—

lit by stars sacrificing herself as a soliloquy to stars

in words made of stars about him being cut to stars

The Kiss

—Amor condusse noi ad una morte.

Inferno, canto V

A girl tells a story to a poet in hell.

The story moves forward, sculpted in stone.

The moment of possession not represented.

Rather, the one right after or right before.

Fictions inside each messenger desire.

Man's illusion resting on a virgin's hip.

Less than forever meets the eye. What is a kiss—

just a flutter? It is the act of recollecting

what almost did happen.

Postcards from Paris

I.

Dear_____,

I bring my pain here, to feel it. To walk on smooth, apple-sized cobblestones. How they soothe. And the food, and the *chocolat chaud*. Music everywhere: jazz and solo cello and rap. But don't get me wrong. The same suffering is here: heartbroken people never getting what they need. It's just that at dusk, in the dark pink air, the swallows tell each other once again what they know. Then the toy boat vendor packs up his cart in the Jardin du Luxembourg. Footsteps across grass. There is no better color than everyone falling silent. Wish everyone were here.

II.

Dear _____,

I remain too afraid to descend into the Catacombs. Who can fathom the dark and damp? I hear that people arranged skulls into a huge heart shape, kept in place by stacks of tibias. (This was hundreds of years ago.) Cavernous palette of grey and white; holes for eyes. Holes never stop watching: beggar, thief, prostitute, prince. I will wait a while for shades and bones. Better to stroll up here, near the Seine and toll of bells, to taste a hint of ash in fresh air. I might walk in a garden so large. Or send this, and wish you were here. Now the rose beginning of rain.

III.

Dear ____,

All I want is to find my place on a green velvet bench inside *La Contrescarpe*,

then slowly make my way toward the Pont Royal. That sweep of stone

over the river, like a gown. Scent of Normandy butter in the air.

People walking around wide-eyed. It is so crucial to save up enough to fly.

Echo

My ache for you then—

               a breeze moving low over the sea.

My ache for you now—

               a breeze moving low over the sea.

La Cravate

Forever transported, the day I learned my dad had died.
Even though he was ill & anyway, isn't death always expected.
Grief is a stun gun—front & center between the eyes. I fly
into a cloud in the air. My mother & sister pick me up on land.
(My sister and I had been estranged, but silver threads now tie
us back together, like the lining of some unseen coat, vast as the sky,
or those ties that bind—the way that old hymn says.) In the car
there is unexpected talk of Charon carrying souls across the Styx.
My sister, driving, cranes her neck to look at me. My mother—
tiny passenger, knot of desperation at her throat. In their home,
his presence everywhere: shoes & jazz, pills to fix him,
the last necktie he wore. I take that tie, without asking my mother.
(If this were a proper sonnet, there would be something tying
all of these verses together, in an effort at dressing them up, right here.)

Further Notes on Your Absence

(Not to mention the fear of not getting it right, not doing it right—
this work of mourning.)   If I don't grieve perfectly, fully—hanging

each clean piece of loss on the line of consciousness, like laundry;
inspecting its various forms, the way elephants hold & worry

every bone of their departed—then what?   Would this night stretch far
to fade every innocence, even these yellow leaves pouring in autumn rain?

(Then, absolutely no more motion. Then, to quote a great poet,
everything close to my face is stone.)   Dad, please let these lines

reveal my smallest certainty—it is not that I think having lost you
might break me.   Rather, it is that still losing you might not.

For my Father, on my Birthday

It is my birthday & you are gone.

You turned yourself into ash & bits of bone

nearly six months ago. It was quite a feat—

simple & humble as a baby being born.

Today your lost bride sings from afar.

Across a great distance, she & I mourn.

A part of her went with you. A part of me did too.

Out of time to that place untold.

This day & this life full of your nowhere

everywhere—silver fog & beat of cold.

Perfect Words

Eight months since you died. I have not cried

over you like I did in winter. Now grief plays

new music: feeling bad about feeling better.

It is April. It is the time for all lilies—

pure trumpets, notes of perfume silence.

You remain ash under immoveable rock.

I hear what you keep saying, from your world

with no clock. Your perfect words urge me:

Daughter with breath go on, even though I am gone.

Wishful Thinking

If only I could touch you (dear reader)

your hands without words, empty as paper.

If only love didn't turn on a dime

every time, or wings were made

of iron   not feathers or wax.

If only your shadow could speak

blue hope arriving soon—these lines

an animal in snow, leaving no tracks.

Penelope's Dream

I am no longer waiting; I am done undoing the seams & threads

of everyday living, after mute dusk comes. All of my adventures

fit in my silver thimble. I have pricked my finger with my needle

too many times. Seen the blood. What would I say to a man broken

beyond all recognition—love's loyal tremble in blind disguise, his face

a mask with paper eyes? Is every form of fire a necessary illusion?

No, let him stay gone. The only home I will ever find is this dream.

Its force enters me now, an exact language of fruit & light. It is all I need.

Le Bonheur

Trust that its little ways will happen—

a clutch of bright tulips, a new poem,

a library book heavy in hand with

its odor of dust. Trust that warmth

comes back to the earth after death—

the faint bird having been returned

to its nest, clean linen in the bed,

this silence joining this line of breath.

J ulia Caroline Knowlton is Professor of French at Agnes Scott College in Atlanta. She holds MA and PhD degrees in French Literature and an MFA from Antioch U. in Los Angeles. She is the author of the memoir *Body Story* and the poetry chapbook *The Café of Unintelligible Desire*. She was named a 2018 Georgia Author of the Year for her chapbook, in a state-wide competition that required a nomination. The recipient of an Academy of American Poets College Prize and a Pushcart nominee, her poems have appeared in numerous literary journals. You may reach her at juliacarolinefr@gmail.com.